50 Dairy-Free Desserts for Every Occasion

By: Kelly Johnson

Table of Contents

- Chocolate Avocado Mousse
- Coconut Milk Rice Pudding
- Almond Flour Chocolate Chip Cookies
- Vegan Chocolate Cake
- Banana Oatmeal Cookies
- Coconut Whipped Cream
- Dairy-Free Chocolate Ice Cream
- Strawberry Coconut Chia Pudding
- Lemon Sorbet
- Chocolate Peanut Butter Cups
- Mango Coconut Panna Cotta
- Vegan Pumpkin Pie
- Berry Coconut Popsicles
- Almond Joy Energy Bites
- Dairy-Free Cheesecake with Cashew Cream
- Chocolate Coconut Macaroons
- Pineapple Coconut Upside-Down Cake
- Peanut Butter Banana Bread
- Raspberry Almond Crumble Bars
- Sweet Potato Brownies
- Chocolate Avocado Brownies
- Coconut Flour Cookies
- Blackberry Sorbet
- Date and Walnut Balls
- Vegan Tiramisu
- Choco-Coconut Bliss Balls
- Chocolate Banana Nice Cream
- Lemon Coconut Bars
- Cashew Cream Fruit Tart
- Pumpkin Coconut Muffins
- Chocolate Almond Butter Fudge
- Vanilla Almond Pudding
- Chocolate Dipped Fruit
- Coconut Chia Seed Pudding
- Berry Parfait with Coconut Yogurt

- Caramel Apple Nachos
- Oatmeal Raisin Cookies
- Mango Coconut Popsicles
- Vegan Chocolate Chip Blondies
- Chocolate Coconut Cream Pie
- Matcha Green Tea Ice Cream
- Lemon Poppy Seed Muffins
- Chocolate Avocado Cake
- Almond Joy Smoothie Bowl
- Raspberry Coconut Energy Balls
- Peanut Butter Chocolate Energy Bites
- Vegan S'mores Bars
- Apple Cinnamon Oatmeal Bake
- Chocolate Chip Zucchini Bread
- Maple Pecan Pie Bars

Chocolate Avocado Mousse

Ingredients:

- 2 ripe avocados
- 1/2 cup cocoa powder
- 1/2 cup maple syrup or agave nectar
- 1/4 cup almond milk
- 1 tsp vanilla extract
- Pinch of salt

Instructions:

1. **Blend ingredients**: In a food processor, combine avocados, cocoa powder, maple syrup, almond milk, vanilla extract, and salt.
2. **Process until smooth**: Blend until the mixture is creamy and smooth, scraping down the sides as needed.
3. **Chill**: Spoon into serving dishes and refrigerate for at least 30 minutes before serving.

Coconut Milk Rice Pudding

Ingredients:

- 1 cup Arborio rice
- 2 cups coconut milk
- 2 cups water
- 1/2 cup maple syrup
- 1 tsp vanilla extract
- 1/2 tsp cinnamon
- Pinch of salt

Instructions:

1. **Cook rice**: In a pot, combine rice, coconut milk, water, maple syrup, vanilla extract, cinnamon, and salt.
2. **Simmer**: Bring to a boil, then reduce heat and simmer for about 20-25 minutes until rice is tender and mixture thickens.
3. **Serve**: Remove from heat and let it cool slightly before serving.

Almond Flour Chocolate Chip Cookies

Ingredients:

- 2 cups almond flour
- 1/2 tsp baking soda
- 1/4 tsp salt
- 1/4 cup coconut oil, melted
- 1/4 cup maple syrup
- 1 tsp vanilla extract
- 1/2 cup dairy-free chocolate chips

Instructions:

1. **Preheat oven**: Preheat the oven to 350°F (175°C) and line a baking sheet with parchment paper.
2. **Mix dry ingredients**: In a bowl, combine almond flour, baking soda, and salt.
3. **Combine wet ingredients**: In another bowl, whisk together melted coconut oil, maple syrup, and vanilla.
4. **Form dough**: Mix wet and dry ingredients until combined, then fold in chocolate chips.
5. **Bake**: Drop spoonfuls of dough onto the baking sheet and bake for 10-12 minutes until golden.

Vegan Chocolate Cake

Ingredients:

- 1 1/2 cups all-purpose flour
- 1 cup cocoa powder
- 1 cup sugar
- 1 tsp baking soda
- 1/2 tsp salt
- 1 cup almond milk
- 1/2 cup vegetable oil
- 1 tbsp apple cider vinegar
- 1 tsp vanilla extract

Instructions:

1. **Preheat oven**: Preheat the oven to 350°F (175°C) and grease two 9-inch cake pans.
2. **Combine dry ingredients**: In a large bowl, mix flour, cocoa powder, sugar, baking soda, and salt.
3. **Mix wet ingredients**: In another bowl, combine almond milk, oil, vinegar, and vanilla.
4. **Combine**: Add wet ingredients to dry ingredients and mix until smooth.
5. **Bake**: Pour batter into prepared pans and bake for 30-35 minutes. Let cool before frosting.

Banana Oatmeal Cookies

Ingredients:

- 2 ripe bananas, mashed
- 1 cup rolled oats
- 1/2 cup almond butter
- 1/4 cup chocolate chips (dairy-free)
- 1/2 tsp cinnamon
- Pinch of salt

Instructions:

1. **Preheat oven**: Preheat the oven to 350°F (175°C) and line a baking sheet with parchment paper.
2. **Mix ingredients**: In a bowl, combine mashed bananas, oats, almond butter, chocolate chips, cinnamon, and salt.
3. **Form cookies**: Drop spoonfuls of the mixture onto the baking sheet.
4. **Bake**: Bake for 12-15 minutes until set and lightly golden.

Coconut Whipped Cream

Ingredients:

- 1 can full-fat coconut milk, chilled
- 2 tbsp powdered sugar
- 1 tsp vanilla extract

Instructions:

1. **Chill coconut milk**: Refrigerate the can of coconut milk overnight.
2. **Scoop cream**: Open the can and scoop out the solid cream into a mixing bowl, leaving the liquid behind.
3. **Whip**: Add powdered sugar and vanilla extract, then whip until fluffy and creamy.

Dairy-Free Chocolate Ice Cream

Ingredients:

- 2 cups coconut milk
- 1/2 cup cocoa powder
- 1/2 cup maple syrup
- 1 tsp vanilla extract
- Pinch of salt

Instructions:

1. **Combine ingredients**: In a bowl, whisk together coconut milk, cocoa powder, maple syrup, vanilla, and salt.
2. **Chill mixture**: Refrigerate for about 30 minutes until cold.
3. **Churn**: Pour the mixture into an ice cream maker and churn according to the manufacturer's instructions.
4. **Freeze**: Transfer to a container and freeze for several hours until firm.

Strawberry Coconut Chia Pudding

Ingredients:

- 1 cup coconut milk
- 1/4 cup chia seeds
- 2 tbsp maple syrup
- 1 cup strawberries, chopped

Instructions:

1. **Combine ingredients**: In a bowl, whisk together coconut milk, chia seeds, and maple syrup.
2. **Refrigerate**: Cover and refrigerate for at least 4 hours or overnight until thickened.
3. **Serve**: Layer the chia pudding with chopped strawberries in serving glasses.

Feel free to ask if you need more recipes or any additional information!

Lemon Sorbet

Ingredients:

- 1 cup fresh lemon juice
- 1 cup water
- 3/4 cup sugar
- Zest of 1 lemon

Instructions:

1. **Make syrup**: In a saucepan, combine water and sugar over medium heat. Stir until the sugar dissolves, then remove from heat.
2. **Combine ingredients**: Stir in lemon juice and lemon zest.
3. **Chill mixture**: Let the mixture cool, then refrigerate for at least 2 hours.
4. **Churn**: Pour the mixture into an ice cream maker and churn according to the manufacturer's instructions. Freeze until firm.

Chocolate Peanut Butter Cups

Ingredients:

- 1 cup dairy-free chocolate chips
- 1/2 cup natural peanut butter
- 2 tbsp maple syrup
- 1/4 cup chopped nuts (optional)

Instructions:

1. **Melt chocolate**: Melt chocolate chips in a microwave or double boiler.
2. **Prepare cups**: Line a muffin tin with cupcake liners and pour a small amount of melted chocolate into each liner.
3. **Add filling**: In a bowl, mix peanut butter and maple syrup. Spoon the mixture into each cup, then top with remaining chocolate.
4. **Chill**: Freeze until solid, about 1 hour.

Mango Coconut Panna Cotta

Ingredients:

- 1 can coconut milk
- 1/4 cup sugar
- 1 tsp vanilla extract
- 1/2 cup mango puree
- 1 tbsp agar-agar powder

Instructions:

1. **Heat coconut milk**: In a saucepan, heat coconut milk, sugar, and vanilla until sugar dissolves.
2. **Add agar-agar**: Sprinkle agar-agar over the mixture and stir to combine. Simmer for 5 minutes.
3. **Set panna cotta**: Pour the mixture into molds and let it cool to room temperature, then refrigerate until set (about 4 hours).
4. **Serve**: Unmold and top with mango puree before serving.

Vegan Pumpkin Pie

Ingredients:

- 1 can pumpkin puree
- 1 cup coconut milk
- 3/4 cup maple syrup
- 1 tsp cinnamon
- 1/2 tsp nutmeg
- 1/4 tsp ginger
- 1/4 tsp salt
- 1 pre-made vegan pie crust

Instructions:

1. **Preheat oven**: Preheat the oven to 350°F (175°C).
2. **Combine filling**: In a bowl, mix pumpkin puree, coconut milk, maple syrup, and spices until smooth.
3. **Fill crust**: Pour the filling into the vegan pie crust.
4. **Bake**: Bake for 45-50 minutes or until set. Let cool before serving.

Berry Coconut Popsicles

Ingredients:

- 1 cup mixed berries (strawberries, blueberries, raspberries)
- 1 cup coconut milk
- 2 tbsp maple syrup

Instructions:

1. **Blend ingredients**: In a blender, combine mixed berries, coconut milk, and maple syrup. Blend until smooth.
2. **Pour into molds**: Pour the mixture into popsicle molds and insert sticks.
3. **Freeze**: Freeze for at least 4 hours or until solid.
4. **Serve**: Remove from molds and enjoy!

Almond Joy Energy Bites

Ingredients:

- 1 cup rolled oats
- 1/2 cup almond butter
- 1/4 cup maple syrup
- 1/2 cup shredded coconut
- 1/4 cup dark chocolate chips
- 1/4 cup chopped almonds

Instructions:

1. **Mix ingredients**: In a bowl, combine all ingredients until well combined.
2. **Form balls**: Roll the mixture into bite-sized balls.
3. **Chill**: Place in the refrigerator for 30 minutes to firm up before serving.

Dairy-Free Cheesecake with Cashew Cream

Ingredients:

- 1 cup cashews (soaked in water for 4 hours)
- 1/4 cup maple syrup
- 1/4 cup coconut oil, melted
- 1 tsp vanilla extract
- 1 pre-made vegan graham cracker crust

Instructions:

1. **Blend cashews**: Drain and rinse soaked cashews, then blend with maple syrup, coconut oil, and vanilla until smooth.
2. **Fill crust**: Pour the cashew mixture into the vegan graham cracker crust.
3. **Chill**: Refrigerate for at least 4 hours until set before serving.

Chocolate Coconut Macaroons

Ingredients:

- 2 cups shredded coconut
- 1/2 cup almond flour
- 1/4 cup cocoa powder
- 1/2 cup maple syrup
- 1 tsp vanilla extract

Instructions:

1. **Preheat oven**: Preheat the oven to 350°F (175°C) and line a baking sheet with parchment paper.
2. **Mix ingredients**: In a bowl, combine all ingredients until well mixed.
3. **Form macaroons**: Scoop tablespoons of the mixture onto the baking sheet.
4. **Bake**: Bake for 15-20 minutes until lightly golden. Let cool before serving.

Feel free to ask if you need more recipes or any additional information!

Pineapple Coconut Upside-Down Cake

Ingredients:

- 1 can pineapple slices (in juice)
- 1/4 cup brown sugar
- 1/4 cup coconut oil (melted)
- 1 cup all-purpose flour
- 1/2 cup sugar
- 1/2 cup coconut milk
- 2 eggs
- 1 tsp baking powder
- 1/2 tsp salt
- 1/2 cup shredded coconut

Instructions:

1. **Preheat oven**: Preheat the oven to 350°F (175°C).
2. **Prepare topping**: In a round cake pan, mix brown sugar and melted coconut oil. Arrange pineapple slices on top and sprinkle with shredded coconut.
3. **Make batter**: In a bowl, whisk together flour, sugar, coconut milk, eggs, baking powder, and salt until smooth.
4. **Combine**: Pour the batter over the pineapple and coconut layer.
5. **Bake**: Bake for 30-35 minutes or until a toothpick comes out clean. Let cool before inverting onto a plate.

Peanut Butter Banana Bread

Ingredients:

- 2 ripe bananas (mashed)
- 1/2 cup peanut butter
- 1/4 cup honey or maple syrup
- 1/4 cup almond milk
- 1 cup all-purpose flour
- 1/2 tsp baking soda
- 1/2 tsp baking powder
- 1/4 tsp salt

Instructions:

1. **Preheat oven**: Preheat the oven to 350°F (175°C) and grease a loaf pan.
2. **Mix wet ingredients**: In a bowl, combine mashed bananas, peanut butter, honey, and almond milk.
3. **Combine dry ingredients**: In another bowl, mix flour, baking soda, baking powder, and salt.
4. **Combine all**: Gradually add the dry ingredients to the wet ingredients, mixing until just combined.
5. **Bake**: Pour the batter into the prepared loaf pan and bake for 45-50 minutes. Let cool before slicing.

Raspberry Almond Crumble Bars

Ingredients:

- 1 cup almond flour
- 1/2 cup oats
- 1/4 cup coconut oil (melted)
- 1/4 cup honey or maple syrup
- 1 cup fresh or frozen raspberries
- 1/4 cup sliced almonds
- 1 tsp vanilla extract
- 1/2 tsp salt

Instructions:

1. **Preheat oven**: Preheat the oven to 350°F (175°C) and line an 8x8-inch baking pan with parchment paper.
2. **Make crust**: In a bowl, combine almond flour, oats, melted coconut oil, honey, and salt. Press half of the mixture into the bottom of the pan.
3. **Add raspberries**: Layer raspberries over the crust and sprinkle with the remaining crumble mixture.
4. **Top with almonds**: Sprinkle sliced almonds on top.
5. **Bake**: Bake for 25-30 minutes until golden. Let cool before cutting into bars.

Sweet Potato Brownies

Ingredients:

- 1 cup mashed sweet potatoes (cooked)
- 1/2 cup almond flour
- 1/2 cup cocoa powder
- 1/4 cup maple syrup
- 1/4 cup coconut oil (melted)
- 1 tsp vanilla extract
- 1/2 tsp baking soda
- 1/4 tsp salt

Instructions:

1. **Preheat oven**: Preheat the oven to 350°F (175°C) and grease an 8x8-inch baking pan.
2. **Mix wet ingredients**: In a bowl, combine mashed sweet potatoes, maple syrup, coconut oil, and vanilla.
3. **Combine dry ingredients**: In another bowl, whisk together almond flour, cocoa powder, baking soda, and salt.
4. **Combine all**: Gradually add the dry ingredients to the wet ingredients and mix until smooth.
5. **Bake**: Pour the batter into the prepared pan and bake for 25-30 minutes. Let cool before slicing.

Chocolate Avocado Brownies

Ingredients:

- 1 ripe avocado (mashed)
- 1/2 cup cocoa powder
- 1/4 cup honey or maple syrup
- 1/4 cup almond butter
- 1/2 tsp vanilla extract
- 1/4 tsp baking powder
- 1/4 tsp salt

Instructions:

1. **Preheat oven**: Preheat the oven to 350°F (175°C) and grease an 8x8-inch baking pan.
2. **Mix ingredients**: In a bowl, combine mashed avocado, cocoa powder, honey, almond butter, vanilla, baking powder, and salt until smooth.
3. **Bake**: Pour the batter into the prepared pan and bake for 20-25 minutes. Let cool before slicing.

Coconut Flour Cookies

Ingredients:

- 1/2 cup coconut flour
- 1/4 cup coconut oil (melted)
- 1/4 cup honey or maple syrup
- 2 eggs
- 1 tsp vanilla extract
- 1/4 tsp baking soda
- 1/4 tsp salt

Instructions:

1. **Preheat oven**: Preheat the oven to 350°F (175°C) and line a baking sheet with parchment paper.
2. **Mix ingredients**: In a bowl, combine coconut flour, melted coconut oil, honey, eggs, vanilla, baking soda, and salt until well mixed.
3. **Form cookies**: Scoop tablespoons of dough onto the baking sheet.
4. **Bake**: Bake for 10-12 minutes until lightly golden. Let cool before serving.

Blackberry Sorbet

Ingredients:

- 2 cups fresh or frozen blackberries
- 1/2 cup sugar
- 1/2 cup water
- 1 tbsp lemon juice

Instructions:

1. **Make syrup**: In a saucepan, combine sugar and water over medium heat until sugar dissolves. Let cool.
2. **Blend ingredients**: In a blender, combine blackberries, syrup, and lemon juice. Blend until smooth.
3. **Chill mixture**: Refrigerate the mixture for at least 1 hour.
4. **Churn**: Pour into an ice cream maker and churn according to the manufacturer's instructions. Freeze until firm.

Date and Walnut Balls

Ingredients:

- 1 cup pitted dates
- 1/2 cup walnuts
- 1/4 cup shredded coconut
- 1 tsp vanilla extract
- Pinch of salt

Instructions:

1. **Blend ingredients**: In a food processor, combine dates, walnuts, shredded coconut, vanilla, and salt. Pulse until the mixture is sticky.
2. **Form balls**: Roll the mixture into small balls.
3. **Chill**: Refrigerate for 30 minutes before serving.

Feel free to ask if you need more recipes or further assistance!

Vegan Tiramisu

Ingredients:

- 1 cup strong brewed coffee (cooled)
- 1/2 cup coconut cream
- 1/4 cup maple syrup
- 1 tsp vanilla extract
- 1 cup almond flour
- 1/4 cup cocoa powder
- 1/2 tsp cinnamon
- Pinch of salt
- Dark chocolate shavings (for garnish)

Instructions:

1. **Prepare coffee mixture**: In a shallow dish, mix cooled coffee with 2 tablespoons of maple syrup.
2. **Make cream layer**: In a bowl, combine coconut cream, remaining maple syrup, and vanilla extract. Mix until smooth.
3. **Assemble layers**: Dip almond flour cookies briefly in the coffee mixture and layer them in a dish. Spread half of the cream mixture on top. Repeat layers.
4. **Chill**: Refrigerate for at least 4 hours. Before serving, dust with cocoa powder and garnish with chocolate shavings.

Choco-Coconut Bliss Balls

Ingredients:

- 1 cup dates (pitted)
- 1/2 cup almond flour
- 1/4 cup cocoa powder
- 1/4 cup shredded coconut
- 1/4 cup almond butter
- 1 tsp vanilla extract
- Pinch of salt

Instructions:

1. **Blend ingredients**: In a food processor, combine all ingredients and blend until a sticky dough forms.
2. **Form balls**: Roll the mixture into small balls.
3. **Coat in coconut**: Roll each ball in shredded coconut if desired.
4. **Chill**: Refrigerate for 30 minutes before serving.

Chocolate Banana Nice Cream

Ingredients:

- 3 ripe bananas (sliced and frozen)
- 1/4 cup cocoa powder
- 2 tbsp almond milk (or any plant milk)
- 1 tsp vanilla extract

Instructions:

1. **Blend ingredients**: In a blender or food processor, combine frozen bananas, cocoa powder, almond milk, and vanilla. Blend until creamy.
2. **Serve immediately**: Enjoy immediately as soft serve or freeze for 1-2 hours for a firmer texture.

Lemon Coconut Bars

Ingredients:

- 1 cup almond flour
- 1/4 cup coconut oil (melted)
- 1/4 cup maple syrup
- 1/2 cup coconut cream
- 1/4 cup lemon juice
- 1 tbsp lemon zest
- 1/4 tsp salt

Instructions:

1. **Preheat oven**: Preheat the oven to 350°F (175°C) and line an 8x8-inch baking pan with parchment paper.
2. **Make crust**: In a bowl, mix almond flour, melted coconut oil, and maple syrup until crumbly. Press into the bottom of the pan.
3. **Prepare filling**: In another bowl, mix coconut cream, lemon juice, lemon zest, and salt until smooth. Pour over the crust.
4. **Bake**: Bake for 20-25 minutes. Let cool before cutting into bars.

Cashew Cream Fruit Tart

Ingredients:

- 1 cup raw cashews (soaked for 4 hours)
- 1/4 cup maple syrup
- 1/4 cup coconut oil (melted)
- 1 tsp vanilla extract
- Fresh fruits (for topping)
- 1 pre-made tart crust (or homemade almond flour crust)

Instructions:

1. **Blend cashew cream**: Drain and rinse soaked cashews. Blend with maple syrup, melted coconut oil, and vanilla until smooth and creamy.
2. **Assemble tart**: Pour the cashew cream into the tart crust and smooth the top.
3. **Top with fruit**: Arrange fresh fruits on top as desired.
4. **Chill**: Refrigerate for at least 2 hours before serving.

Pumpkin Coconut Muffins

Ingredients:

- 1 cup pumpkin puree
- 1/2 cup coconut flour
- 1/4 cup maple syrup
- 1/4 cup coconut oil (melted)
- 2 eggs (or flax eggs)
- 1 tsp baking soda
- 1 tsp pumpkin spice
- Pinch of salt

Instructions:

1. **Preheat oven**: Preheat the oven to 350°F (175°C) and line a muffin tin with liners.
2. **Mix wet ingredients**: In a bowl, combine pumpkin puree, maple syrup, melted coconut oil, and eggs.
3. **Combine dry ingredients**: In another bowl, mix coconut flour, baking soda, pumpkin spice, and salt.
4. **Combine all**: Gradually add dry ingredients to the wet ingredients and mix until just combined.
5. **Bake**: Fill muffin liners and bake for 20-25 minutes. Let cool before serving.

Chocolate Almond Butter Fudge

Ingredients:

- 1/2 cup almond butter
- 1/4 cup cocoa powder
- 1/4 cup maple syrup
- 1/4 cup coconut oil (melted)
- Pinch of salt

Instructions:

1. **Mix ingredients**: In a bowl, combine almond butter, cocoa powder, maple syrup, melted coconut oil, and salt. Stir until smooth.
2. **Pour into pan**: Pour the mixture into a lined small baking dish and smooth the top.
3. **Chill**: Refrigerate until firm (about 2 hours). Cut into squares before serving.

Vanilla Almond Pudding

Ingredients:

- 1/2 cup almond milk
- 1/4 cup almond flour
- 2 tbsp maple syrup
- 1 tbsp cornstarch
- 1 tsp vanilla extract
- Pinch of salt

Instructions:

1. **Combine ingredients**: In a saucepan, whisk together almond milk, almond flour, maple syrup, cornstarch, vanilla, and salt.
2. **Cook mixture**: Cook over medium heat, stirring constantly, until thickened (about 5 minutes).
3. **Chill**: Pour into serving dishes and refrigerate until set. Serve chilled.

Feel free to reach out if you need more recipes or any further assistance!

Chocolate Dipped Fruit

Ingredients:

- 1 cup dark chocolate chips
- 1 tbsp coconut oil
- Assorted fruits (strawberries, bananas, apple slices, etc.)
- Optional toppings (crushed nuts, shredded coconut)

Instructions:

1. **Melt chocolate**: In a microwave-safe bowl, combine chocolate chips and coconut oil. Microwave in 30-second intervals until melted and smooth.
2. **Dip fruit**: Dip each piece of fruit into the melted chocolate, allowing excess to drip off.
3. **Add toppings**: If desired, roll in optional toppings before placing on parchment paper.
4. **Chill**: Refrigerate for 30 minutes or until chocolate is set.

Coconut Chia Seed Pudding

Ingredients:

- 1/2 cup chia seeds
- 2 cups coconut milk
- 1/4 cup maple syrup (or to taste)
- 1 tsp vanilla extract
- Fresh fruit (for topping)

Instructions:

1. **Combine ingredients**: In a bowl, mix chia seeds, coconut milk, maple syrup, and vanilla until well combined.
2. **Refrigerate**: Cover and refrigerate for at least 4 hours or overnight until thickened.
3. **Serve**: Stir well before serving and top with fresh fruit.

Berry Parfait with Coconut Yogurt

Ingredients:

- 2 cups coconut yogurt
- 2 cups mixed berries (strawberries, blueberries, raspberries)
- 1/4 cup granola
- 2 tbsp maple syrup (optional)

Instructions:

1. **Layer ingredients**: In glasses or bowls, layer coconut yogurt, mixed berries, and granola.
2. **Repeat layers**: Repeat the layers until ingredients are used up.
3. **Drizzle syrup**: If desired, drizzle with maple syrup before serving.

Caramel Apple Nachos

Ingredients:

- 2 apples (sliced)
- 1/4 cup almond butter (or any nut butter)
- 1/4 cup dairy-free caramel sauce
- 2 tbsp chopped nuts (optional)
- 1/4 cup chocolate chips (optional)

Instructions:

1. **Arrange apple slices**: Lay apple slices on a plate.
2. **Drizzle toppings**: Drizzle almond butter and caramel sauce over the apples.
3. **Add nuts and chocolate**: Sprinkle with nuts and chocolate chips if desired.

Oatmeal Raisin Cookies

Ingredients:

- 1 cup rolled oats
- 1/2 cup almond flour
- 1/2 cup maple syrup
- 1/4 cup coconut oil (melted)
- 1/2 cup raisins
- 1 tsp cinnamon
- 1 tsp vanilla extract
- 1/2 tsp baking soda
- Pinch of salt

Instructions:

1. **Preheat oven**: Preheat the oven to 350°F (175°C) and line a baking sheet with parchment paper.
2. **Mix wet ingredients**: In a bowl, combine melted coconut oil, maple syrup, and vanilla extract.
3. **Combine dry ingredients**: In another bowl, mix oats, almond flour, cinnamon, baking soda, and salt.
4. **Mix all ingredients**: Combine wet and dry ingredients and fold in raisins.
5. **Scoop cookies**: Drop spoonfuls of dough onto the prepared baking sheet.
6. **Bake**: Bake for 12-15 minutes until golden. Let cool before serving.

Mango Coconut Popsicles

Ingredients:

- 2 ripe mangoes (peeled and diced)
- 1 cup coconut milk
- 2 tbsp honey or maple syrup (optional)

Instructions:

1. **Blend ingredients**: In a blender, combine diced mangoes, coconut milk, and honey (if using). Blend until smooth.
2. **Pour into molds**: Pour the mixture into popsicle molds.
3. **Freeze**: Insert sticks and freeze for at least 4 hours or until solid.
4. **Serve**: To remove, run warm water over the outside of the molds for a few seconds.

Vegan Chocolate Chip Blondies

Ingredients:

- 1 cup almond flour
- 1/2 cup almond butter
- 1/4 cup maple syrup
- 1/4 cup coconut sugar
- 1 tsp vanilla extract
- 1/2 tsp baking soda
- 1/4 cup dairy-free chocolate chips

Instructions:

1. **Preheat oven**: Preheat the oven to 350°F (175°C) and line an 8x8-inch baking dish with parchment paper.
2. **Mix wet ingredients**: In a bowl, combine almond butter, maple syrup, coconut sugar, and vanilla extract.
3. **Combine dry ingredients**: Add almond flour and baking soda, mixing until just combined. Fold in chocolate chips.
4. **Pour into pan**: Spread the mixture evenly in the prepared baking dish.
5. **Bake**: Bake for 20-25 minutes until golden. Let cool before cutting into squares.

Chocolate Coconut Cream Pie

Ingredients:

- 1 pre-made pie crust
- 1 can coconut cream (chilled)
- 1/4 cup cocoa powder
- 1/2 cup powdered sugar (or to taste)
- 1 tsp vanilla extract
- Chocolate shavings (for garnish)

Instructions:

1. **Make filling**: In a bowl, whip chilled coconut cream until fluffy. Gradually add cocoa powder, powdered sugar, and vanilla, mixing until smooth.
2. **Fill crust**: Pour the chocolate coconut cream filling into the pie crust and smooth the top.
3. **Chill**: Refrigerate for at least 2 hours before serving.
4. **Garnish**: Before serving, top with chocolate shavings.

Feel free to ask if you need more recipes or any further assistance!

Matcha Green Tea Ice Cream

Ingredients:

- 1 cup coconut milk
- 1 cup almond milk
- 1/2 cup maple syrup
- 2 tbsp matcha green tea powder
- 1 tsp vanilla extract
- Pinch of salt

Instructions:

1. **Combine ingredients**: In a mixing bowl, whisk together coconut milk, almond milk, maple syrup, matcha powder, vanilla extract, and salt until smooth.
2. **Chill mixture**: Refrigerate for at least 1 hour to chill.
3. **Churn ice cream**: Pour the mixture into an ice cream maker and churn according to the manufacturer's instructions until it reaches a soft-serve consistency.
4. **Freeze**: Transfer to an airtight container and freeze for at least 4 hours before serving.

Lemon Poppy Seed Muffins

Ingredients:

- 1 1/2 cups all-purpose flour
- 1/2 cup sugar
- 2 tsp poppy seeds
- 1 tsp baking powder
- 1/2 tsp baking soda
- 1/4 tsp salt
- 1/2 cup almond milk
- 1/3 cup vegetable oil
- 1 tbsp lemon zest
- 1/4 cup lemon juice
- 1 tsp vanilla extract

Instructions:

1. **Preheat oven**: Preheat the oven to 350°F (175°C) and line a muffin tin with paper liners.
2. **Mix dry ingredients**: In a large bowl, combine flour, sugar, poppy seeds, baking powder, baking soda, and salt.
3. **Mix wet ingredients**: In another bowl, whisk together almond milk, oil, lemon zest, lemon juice, and vanilla extract.
4. **Combine mixtures**: Pour the wet ingredients into the dry ingredients and stir until just combined.
5. **Bake**: Fill the muffin cups 2/3 full and bake for 18-20 minutes or until a toothpick comes out clean.

Chocolate Avocado Cake

Ingredients:

- 1 1/2 cups almond flour
- 1/2 cup cocoa powder
- 1/2 cup maple syrup
- 1/2 cup ripe avocado (mashed)
- 1/4 cup almond milk
- 1 tsp baking soda
- 1/2 tsp salt
- 1 tsp vanilla extract

Instructions:

1. **Preheat oven**: Preheat the oven to 350°F (175°C) and grease a 9-inch round cake pan.
2. **Mix dry ingredients**: In a bowl, combine almond flour, cocoa powder, baking soda, and salt.
3. **Mix wet ingredients**: In another bowl, mix avocado, maple syrup, almond milk, and vanilla until smooth.
4. **Combine mixtures**: Add the wet ingredients to the dry ingredients and stir until just combined.
5. **Bake**: Pour the batter into the prepared pan and bake for 25-30 minutes, or until a toothpick comes out clean.

Almond Joy Smoothie Bowl

Ingredients:

- 1 banana (frozen)
- 1 cup almond milk
- 2 tbsp almond butter
- 2 tbsp cocoa powder
- 1 tbsp shredded coconut
- Toppings: sliced almonds, chocolate chips, coconut flakes

Instructions:

1. **Blend ingredients**: In a blender, combine frozen banana, almond milk, almond butter, cocoa powder, and shredded coconut. Blend until smooth and creamy.
2. **Serve**: Pour into a bowl and top with sliced almonds, chocolate chips, and additional coconut flakes.

Raspberry Coconut Energy Balls

Ingredients:

- 1 cup oats
- 1/2 cup almond butter
- 1/2 cup shredded coconut
- 1/2 cup raspberries (fresh or frozen)
- 2 tbsp maple syrup
- 1 tsp vanilla extract

Instructions:

1. **Combine ingredients**: In a bowl, mix oats, almond butter, shredded coconut, raspberries, maple syrup, and vanilla until well combined.
2. **Form balls**: Roll the mixture into small balls, about 1 inch in diameter.
3. **Chill**: Place in the refrigerator for at least 30 minutes to set.

Peanut Butter Chocolate Energy Bites

Ingredients:

- 1 cup oats
- 1/2 cup peanut butter
- 1/4 cup honey or maple syrup
- 1/4 cup chocolate chips
- 1 tsp vanilla extract

Instructions:

1. **Mix ingredients**: In a bowl, combine oats, peanut butter, honey, chocolate chips, and vanilla extract. Stir until well mixed.
2. **Form bites**: Roll the mixture into small balls, about 1 inch in diameter.
3. **Chill**: Place in the refrigerator for at least 30 minutes before serving.

Vegan S'mores Bars

Ingredients:

- 1 cup graham cracker crumbs
- 1/2 cup almond flour
- 1/4 cup coconut oil (melted)
- 1/4 cup maple syrup
- 1 cup dairy-free chocolate chips
- 1 cup mini marshmallows

Instructions:

1. **Preheat oven**: Preheat the oven to 350°F (175°C) and line an 8x8-inch baking dish with parchment paper.
2. **Mix crust**: In a bowl, combine graham cracker crumbs, almond flour, melted coconut oil, and maple syrup until crumbly.
3. **Press into dish**: Press the mixture into the bottom of the prepared baking dish.
4. **Bake**: Bake for 10 minutes, then remove from the oven and sprinkle chocolate chips and mini marshmallows on top.
5. **Broil**: Return to the oven and broil for 1-2 minutes until marshmallows are golden. Allow to cool before cutting into bars.

Apple Cinnamon Oatmeal Bake

Ingredients:

- 2 cups rolled oats
- 2 apples (diced)
- 1/4 cup maple syrup
- 1 tsp cinnamon
- 1/2 tsp baking powder
- 1/2 cup almond milk
- 1/4 cup chopped nuts (optional)

Instructions:

1. **Preheat oven**: Preheat the oven to 350°F (175°C) and grease an 8x8-inch baking dish.
2. **Combine ingredients**: In a bowl, mix oats, diced apples, maple syrup, cinnamon, baking powder, and almond milk until well combined. Fold in nuts if using.
3. **Bake**: Pour the mixture into the prepared baking dish and bake for 25-30 minutes until set and golden.

Feel free to ask if you need more recipes or any further assistance!

Chocolate Chip Zucchini Bread

Ingredients:

- 1 ½ cups grated zucchini (about 1 medium zucchini)
- 1 ½ cups all-purpose flour
- 1 tsp baking powder
- ½ tsp baking soda
- ½ tsp salt
- 1 tsp cinnamon
- ½ cup sugar
- ½ cup brown sugar
- 2 large eggs
- ½ cup vegetable oil
- 1 tsp vanilla extract
- 1 cup chocolate chips

Instructions:

1. **Preheat oven**: Preheat the oven to 350°F (175°C) and grease a 9x5-inch loaf pan.
2. **Mix dry ingredients**: In a bowl, whisk together flour, baking powder, baking soda, salt, and cinnamon.
3. **Mix wet ingredients**: In another bowl, combine grated zucchini, sugar, brown sugar, eggs, oil, and vanilla until smooth.
4. **Combine mixtures**: Add the dry ingredients to the wet ingredients and stir until just combined. Fold in the chocolate chips.
5. **Bake**: Pour the batter into the prepared loaf pan and bake for 50-60 minutes or until a toothpick inserted in the center comes out clean. Let cool before slicing.

Maple Pecan Pie Bars

Ingredients:

- **For the crust:**
    - 1 ½ cups all-purpose flour
    - ½ cup powdered sugar
    - ½ cup unsalted butter (softened)
    - ¼ tsp salt
- **For the filling:**
    - 1 cup pecans (chopped)
    - ¾ cup maple syrup
    - ½ cup brown sugar
    - 3 large eggs
    - 2 tbsp unsalted butter (melted)
    - 1 tsp vanilla extract
    - ½ tsp salt

Instructions:

1. **Preheat oven**: Preheat the oven to 350°F (175°C) and line an 8x8-inch baking pan with parchment paper.
2. **Make the crust**: In a bowl, mix flour, powdered sugar, softened butter, and salt until crumbly. Press the mixture evenly into the bottom of the prepared pan.
3. **Bake the crust**: Bake for 15-20 minutes or until lightly golden.
4. **Prepare the filling**: In a separate bowl, whisk together chopped pecans, maple syrup, brown sugar, eggs, melted butter, vanilla extract, and salt until smooth.
5. **Combine**: Pour the filling over the pre-baked crust and spread evenly.
6. **Bake**: Return to the oven and bake for an additional 25-30 minutes or until the filling is set. Allow to cool completely before cutting into bars.

Let me know if you need more recipes or any other assistance!

www.ingramcontent.com/pod-product-compliance
Lightning Source LLC
LaVergne TN
LVHW081335060526
838201LV00055B/2653